ZIGREX CODEX

RITUALS OF POWER, RESURRECTION AND COMMAND

TANYA KARUMBAIAH

Chennai • Bangalore

CLEVER FOX PUBLISHING
Chennai, India

Published by CLEVER FOX PUBLISHING 2025
Copyright © Tanya Karumbaiah 2025

All Rights Reserved.
ISBN: 978-93-67073-05-6

This book has been published with all reasonable efforts taken to make the material error-free after the consent of the author. No part of this book shall be used, reproduced in any manner whatsoever without written permission from the author, except in the case of brief quotations embodied in critical articles and reviews.

The Author of this book is solely responsible and liable for its content including but not limited to the views, representations, descriptions, statements, information, opinions and references ["Content"]. The Content of this book shall not constitute or be construed or deemed to reflect the opinion or expression of the Publisher or Editor. Neither the Publisher nor Editor endorse or approve the Content of this book or guarantee the reliability, accuracy or completeness of the Content published herein and do not make any representations or warranties of any kind, express or implied, including but not limited to the implied warranties of merchantability, fitness for a particular purpose. The Publisher and Editor shall not be liable whatsoever for any errors, omissions, whether such errors or omissions result from negligence, accident, or any other cause or claims for loss or damages of any kind, including without limitation, indirect or consequential loss or damage arising out of use, inability to use, or about the reliability, accuracy or sufficiency of the information contained in this book.

DEDICATED TO THE UNSEEN ONES

To the wild hearts, broken but burning, who were never chosen, so they chose themselves. This codex is your resurrection.

ACKNOWLEDGEMENT

"My deepest gratitude to my parents—for giving me the foundation of a fine education and upbringing, which shaped my voice, my words, and my world. To Poonacha—my unwavering anchor and quiet strength through every storm and silence. And to Shashikant Khuntia—an unlikely connection who, in passing, planted the first seed that led me to write"

THE CODEX VOW

I vow to use this Codex not for vanity but for *truth*.
To protect my energy like a fortress,
To remember that I am not lost—I am becoming.
To never again kneel before anything that does not recognize my fire.

I vow that everything I write within these pages
will hold power—because **I am power.**

— Signed,
[Your Name Here — or your Alchemist Name]

Date:
Phase: (Waning / Waxing / Dark Moon (choose what phase feels right)

MANIFESTO

The Creed of the Alchemist

> I no longer beg.
> I command.
>
> I do not seek light—I *wield* shadow.
> I do not wait for signs—I *become* the signal.
> I do not worship—I *become* what is worshipped.
>
> I write to reclaim.
> I channel to awaken.
> I walk alone because the throne was made for one.
>
> This Codex is my soul, split open and bound in pages.
> If you dare open it, know this: you are not reading a book.
> You are awakening a storm.

WHO IS THE ZIGREX?

"Zigrex: Reborn from the Blaze"

The sky burned with the fury of a thousand suns, as the earth trembled beneath the weight of destruction. In the heart of the inferno, a tigress, fierce and untamable, succumbed to the flames. Yet, as the embers fell, something stirred in the ashes. From the smoldering ruins, a new being rose—unrecognizable, beyond gender, beyond form. The Zigrex.

A creature of raw power. It did not walk; it glided through the smoke, its presence both terrifying and awe-inspiring. The world trembled as it moved, a force too fierce to contain, a soul forged in the crucible of survival. It exuded an aura of untouchable confidence, its eyes gleaming with the knowing of a thousand battles.

"Do you dare to challenge me?" The Zigrex's voice was a low, guttural growl, vibrating through the air like thunder. "I have burned, and now I rise. Again and again, I will rise."

Vulnerability? It didn't know it. The Zigrex thrived on provocation, every step an assertion of power.

"Pain is my companion, but it is not my master," it whispered, stepping forward. "You think I am broken, but I am whole."

WHO IS THE ZIGREX?

You could feel it before you saw it—a pulse, a tremor in the air. The Zigrex could sense you, miles away, before your shadow even reached its ground. It could see through your lies, smell the deceit on your breath.

"Run," it said softly, though the threat was unspoken but felt like a blade against your skin. "Run fast, but know this: There's no escaping the truth that lies in my gaze."

If you crossed its path, you wouldn't have time to regret it. Run. Run fast. Don't look back. And above all, never meet its gaze.

But the Zigrex wasn't just a force. It was the embodiment of transformation. It was the creature you could become if you dared to shed the skin of who you thought you were. The version of yourself that lies hidden beneath layers of fear, of survival, of the past. It unlocked the power to evolve, to transcend, to rise above.

"I am the spark that will ignite the world," the Zigrex declared, staring at its reflection in the shattered glass of the world. "I have become what I was destined to be, not what they wanted me to be. What will you choose to become?"

Yet, in its very essence, the Zigrex was a paradox. A being of both spiritual hunger and skepticism. It sought meaning, but questioned everything it encountered. It was a seeker of truth, but always with caution, always analyzing. It embraced belief, but only when proof met its gaze.

"Faith without evidence is a lie," it said, looking beyond the horizon. "I will not bend to your gods until I see them in the flesh. Trust is earned, not given."

It was a restless flame, forever learning, transforming. Unconventional, a creator without limits, a mind sharp as steel. moving through the world with discipline and an obsession for excellence rather than perfection. Mediocrity could never hold its interest.

"Perfection is a ghost," the Zigrex scoffed, its voice like a wind that cut through the stillness. "I don't chase what's unattainable. I chase what's real. I strive for excellence because that's what breaks the chains of this world."

Every pulse, every thought, every movement was a step toward mastery.

The Zigrex knew that to rise, it first had to burn. It had been vanquished before, but from that very defeat, it had become something greater. A phoenix forged in struggle, with power born from within.

"Remember this," it said, its voice a whisper now, but one that carried the weight of worlds. "I was nothing once. I was ash. Now, I am everything."

It was a force that understood: to conquer the world, you first had to conquer the soul. And in that victory, everything else would bend.

"Conquer the soul, and the world will follow," the Zigrex proclaimed, its eyes blazing with unyielding certainty. "And in that victory, all will kneel."

INTRODUCTION

(Zigrex Codex: The Alchemist's Journal)

How I Switched from invocation to intention: My Journey from Surrender to Command

I used to think... temples, pariharas, offerings—these would finally fix my life. That if I prayed hard enough, did the right rituals, went to the right places, maybe—just maybe—my life would finally take off. But it never did.

And what broke me wasn't just that things didn't change. It's that I saw other people around me receiving miracles. Someone dreams of Devi Maa, and their pain vanishes. Someone walks from Coorg to Kerala and a divine voice tells them, "Your body is healed,"— and it is. They feel something enter them. They glow. They cry. They say, "I felt God."

And me? Silence. Every time.

Even predictions made about me by the so-called divine people? All wrong. Every. Single. Time. They said I'd get a job. That job would fund my business. Never happened. They couldn't even see that the house I lived in was draining me, blocking me. Nothing they said fit.

And you know what? I get it now.

I wasn't rejected. I was unreadable. I was never meant to be predicted, prophesied, or healed by someone else's system. I wasn't made to follow. I was made to build, to create. To forge something that didn't exist before.

That's why I created ZIGREX.

Zigrex didn't come from incense and faith. It came from blood, silence, and rage. It was born because no God answered. So, I became my own altar.

There was a time when I clung to Vedic mantras like lifelines. Each syllable, each chant—whether it was the powerful Hanuman Chalisa or the fierce Durga Mantra—felt like an offering to something greater. I was taught, like so many of us are, that surrender was sacred. That humility would bring blessings. That repetition would invite divine grace.

And for a while, I believed that.

I practiced with discipline. I chanted with devotion. I breathed through my Pranayama as if each inhale would carry my prayers further.

But somewhere along the line, something began to shift.

I noticed that the more I begged, the less I received. The more I surrendered, the more life demanded. And the more I waited for signs, the more silence I got back.

That's when I knew—I was no longer the same person.

The girl who used to kneel was rising.

It wasn't that I had lost faith. It's that I had found myself.

INTRODUCTION

I realized mantras are beautiful, but they're devotional—they're about surrender, about asking, about hoping. They have clear energy, yes. They protect, purify, and bring structure to chaos. But they don't move reality fast unless you're already karmically aligned. This is something that nobody would tell you.

And I wasn't interested in waiting anymore.

I was interested in being willing.

I didn't want to bow anymore. I wanted to build.

That's when I turned to Codex.

Not the dramatic kind shown in movies. Not the ones filled with superstition or shadows. But clean, focused, elemental rituals—

Codex that are declarations, not requests.

Codex that says, "This is mine." Not "Please, if it's your will…"

I still do Pranayama. Because breath is power, and I use that breath to fuel my will. I still visit temples, especially when I travel. And yes, I occasionally chant mantras like The Hanuman Chalisa—not because I'm begging for protection, but because I honor the divine force as a peer, not a parent. But I no longer mix my paths.

If I'm doing my rituals of dominion, I don't chant mantras that day. Codexes are about self-authority, while mantras are about surrender, and both deserve their own space.

This shift wasn't about rebellion.

It was about recognizing who I've become.

I don't want to be 'chosen' anymore.

INTRODUCTION

I choose myself.

And that? That's the real miracle.

Zigrex isn't a path for the blessed.

It's for the ones who were burned by temples, bruised by rituals, and rose anyway.

There was a time I knelt. I folded my hands, looked up to a sky that never looked back. I prayed until my bones ached, until my voice cracked, until my hope dissolved into silence. But silence became a womb. From it, I was reborn—not as a supplicant, but as a sovereign.

This Codex is not written in ink.

It is carved from every unanswered prayer, every betrayal, every sleepless night that turned me into fire.

This is not a spellbook. This is a relic of reckoning. A journal that breathes, pulses, and obeys no god but will.

This is ZIGREX—not a name.

A force.

THIS IS NOT A SPELLBOOK

(For the One Who Trusts With Doubt)

This is not a spellbook.

This is not some woo-woo nonsense wrapped in glitter and goddess talk.

It's not an invitation to "trust the universe," "surrender," or "raise your vibes" without context or consequence.

This Codex was not made for people who believe blindly. It was made for you, the one who trusts with doubt. The one who has watched faith crumble, hope backfire, and promises rot into silence.

And still, here you are. Reading this.

The Zigrex Codex is not witchcraft.

It's not a religion nor a spiritual platitude

It is a system. A symbolic structure. A psychological ritual for those who need to feel power in their hands again, even if they don't know what to believe in anymore. This is not witchcraft. These are symbolic, psychological, and energetic tools used for focus, intention, and transformation. Just like lighting a candle in prayer or using incense in temples—it's about energy and meaning, not magic or superstition.

WHAT IS IT, THEN?

It's a framework. A mental reprogramming system. A ritualized rewrite of internal chaos.

- The language in this Codex? Designed to override passive thought.
- The symbols, fonts, and visuals? Meant to speak to your subconscious before your logic shoots them down.
- The repetition of ritual? That's where the real magic happens—not outside you, but inside your neurology.

This isn't fiction. It's neuroscience. It's somatic anchoring. It's energetic self-alignment. It's every time you said, "No one is coming to save me"—and then lit the damn candle anyway.

But Will It Change My Destiny?

That depends.

If by "destiny" you mean some cosmic contract sealed in the stars, you might not break it.

But if by destiny you mean the pattern you've lived in—the repeated collapse, the lack, the numbness—then yes. Yes, this can change that.

Because rituals change behavior.

Behavior changes decisions.

Decisions shift outcomes.

And outcomes, repeated enough, become your new fate.

So Why Does It Work—Even If I Don't Believe?

Because belief isn't a requirement.
Willingness is.

Doubt can sit at the altar. Let it.

Approach with intent, voice, breath, and movement, and something will change. Not from magic, but because your nervous system will start to trust you again.

This Codex is not asking you to believe in miracles.

It's asking you to move like you deserve one.

Final Word

You can call this a placebo. You can call this poetic.
But if it gets you to sit in power, even for five minutes, after a lifetime of feeling small, then it's working.

No gods.

No gurus.

Just you.

And the Codex.

And the fire you thought you lost.

WHAT IS IT, THEN?

Before You Begin – The Preparation Rite (Optional but strongly recommended)- Do this at least 10–15 mins before any Zigrex Ritual

1. **Cleanse Your Body:**
   - A quick shower or just washing your face, hands, and feet is enough.
   - You're washing off the noise, the mundane world, stepping into something more intentional.

2. **Dress with Intention:**
   - Wear something comfortable, preferably dark, neutral, or skin-toned.
   - No logos, distractions—this is your presence taking center stage.

3. **Set Your Space:**
   - Wipe the surface you're working on.
   - Dim the lights or light a candle—shift the mood from "everyday" to ritual mode.
   - Keep your ritual items nearby (mirror, salt, sigil, etc.).

4. **Silence the Noise:**
   - Put your phone on silent.
   - Play low ambient sounds if you need, but make this space sacred.

5. **Anchor Your Breath (1 minute):**
   - Close your eyes. Inhale deeply. Exhale slowly. Do it thrice.
   - Say softly: *"I am present. I am potent. I am rising."*
   - It is recommended to begin any ritual with yoga and pranayama to center the body and align the breath with intention

ZIGREX CODEX:
THE ALCHEMIST'S JOURNAL

Chapter I – Invocation of the Flame 1
a. Opening Codex: The Rite of Rekindling 1
b. Candle Flame Command Ritual 3
c. Fire Element Ritual: Burn the Obstacle 5

Chapter II – The Breath Command 7
a. Breath & Will Alignment 7
b. Pranayama Force Integration 9
c. Wind Element Force: Summon the Shift 11

Chapter III – The Waters Within 13
a. Mirror Ritual of the Inner Self 13
b. Invoke Fluid Fortune 15
c. Emotional Alchemy Ritual 16

Chapter IV – Earth & Bone 17
a. Grounding Circle of Protection 17
b. Earth Element Conjuration: Call of the Hidden Gold 19
c. Banishing the Past: Ash & Soil Reversal 20

Chapter V – Rituals of the Shadow Moon 21
a. New Moon: Ritual of Rebirth 21
b. Full Moon: Mirror of Power 23
c. Waning Moon: Cut the Cord 24
d. Waxing Moon: Draw What is Mine 25

Chapter VI – The Money Magnetism Ritual 26
a. Full Ritual (to be unlocked after your 7-day Power Ritual is complete) 26

Chapter VII – Zigrex Seals & Sigils 29
a. Personal Sigil Creation 29
b. Binding Sigils 31
c. Attraction Glyphs 33

Chapter VIII- The final invocation- Zigrex Ascension Rite 35
a. Ritual of the Four Elemental Keys 36
b. Mirror of Becoming Ritual 37
c. Zigrex Oath Ritual 38
d. Flame-Seal Close 39

Chapter IX- Morning Dominion Decree 41
a. 7 versions, one for each day of the week 41

CHAPTER I
INVOCATION OF THE FLAME

Codex 1: The Rite of Rekindling

Where fire meets will, the world begins to tremble.

Purpose: To awaken the primal fire within. This is your initiation Codex — a vow to power.

What You Need:

A black candle

A bowl of salt

A mirror

Your voice (unshaken, raw)

Ritual:

1. Place the mirror before you. Behind it, place the black candle.
2. Draw a circle around you with salt — this is your boundary, your fortress.
3. Breathe in for 4 counts, hold for 4, exhale for 4 — three rounds. Feel your heart begin to drum.

4. Light the candle and stare into the mirror. Let your eyes meet your eyes.
5. Speak aloud (with command):
   "By flame and form,
   By bone and breath,
   I break the chains of silent death.
   Zigrex awakens at my call,
   Let false gods fade, let shadows fall.
   My will is law, my voice the spark,
   I conjure light within the dark."

Hold your gaze. Whisper once: *"So it is spoken. So, it shall burn."*

Let the candle burn for a while. Snuff it (never blow). Gather the salt. Dispose it outside, preferably at a crossroad, base of a tree, or a running stream (not stagnant or drainage water)— you've marked your dominion.

Codex II: The Candle Flame Command Ritual- Dominion of the Flame

Purpose:

To awaken your commanding voice—when the world has ignored you, this ritual lights a fire that cannot be unseen. Use it when you feel unseen, unheard, or when your presence needs to radiate undeniable power.

You Will Need:

- A black candle (for command) or a red candle (for forceful energy)
- A pin or blade to carve
- A piece of paper and a pen
- A fireproof bowl
- A drop of your perfume or oil you associate with self-power

Preparation:

1. Sit in silence. Feel the pulse of everything that ever tried to dim you. Hold it.
2. With the blade or pin, carve a word onto the candle: *"Command"*, *"Rise"*, or your name in capital letters. Then, light your candle.
3. On the paper, write what you demand from the universe. Not what you wish. What do you demand? Be specific. Use direct, powerful language.

Ritual:

1. Hold the paper in your hand. Whisper this:
   I am no longer the seeker. I am the force.
   Fire listens. Shadows obey.
   Let my word strike the unseen and be carried to the ends of the earth.
2. Anoint the paper with your perfume or oil.
3. Burn the paper in the fireproof bowl using the candle's flame.
4. As it burns, stare into the flame and say:
   By fire and fury, I command.
   No more silence. No more delay.
   Let it be done.

Closing:

Let the candle burn until it's done (or snuff it with a lid, never blow it out). Collect the ashes and bury them in soil or keep them in a tiny pouch if you want to carry the command energy with you.

Fire Element Ritual: Burn the Obstacle
Codex III: Classification Ritual

Purpose:

To ignite the fire of transmutation. This Ritual is designed to burn through inner and outer obstacles—energetic blockages, emotional heaviness, external resistance, or self-doubt. Fire does not negotiate; it devours.

You Will Need:

- A fire-safe bowl or cauldron
- A piece of paper
- A pen (preferably red or black ink)
- A candle (orange or red recommended)
- Salt (for circle)
- A matchstick or lighter
- A small amount of dried basil or bay leaf (optional—both are used for clearing)

Ritual Steps:

1. **The Circle of Dominion:**

   Draw a salt circle around your seated space. This is your sacred forge—nothing enters, nothing leaves, unless you will. Sit cross-legged or grounded inside this boundary.

2. **The Flame Awakens:**

   Light the candle. Watch the flame flicker. Let it mirror the flame within you—old, ancient, unrelenting. Speak softly:
   "Flame of origin, keeper of fury, I call upon thee. Burn through what binds, break what clings."

3. **Identify the Obstacle:**
   Write down **exactly** what stands in your way—name it with brutal honesty. Whether it's fear, failure, poverty, betrayal, or a specific person or habit, write it down with full emotional charge. One obstacle per ritual.

4. **Speak the Command:**
   Hold the paper over the flame (not too close yet). Say:
   "You are not greater than me. I name you, I face you, and now—I burn you."

5. **Burn the Obstacle:**
   Light the paper from the candle flame. Place it in the fire-safe bowl and let it burn completely. Watch it disintegrate. Do not flinch. This is you reclaiming dominion.

6. **Ashes to Salt:**
   Once cooled, take a pinch of the ashes and mix them with a bit of salt. This becomes your **Ward Dust**—an energetic mixture of what you overcame and your protection. You can keep it in a pouch, or sprinkle a line outside your door to say:
   "What once bound me now guards me."

7. **Close the Ritual:**
   Extinguish the flame. Whisper:
   "Let what was burnt never return. Let what was blocked now flow. So, it is. So, it shall remain."
   Leave the salt circle undisturbed for one hour. Then gently dismantle it and pour it outside—at a crossroad, under a tree, or in streaming water.

CHAPTER II

THE BREATH COMMAND

Codex 1: Breath & Will Alignment

Purpose:

To awaken the sleeping force of intent within the breath and bind it to the will. This is the first rite of activation for command over personal energy and environmental influence.

Preparation:

Find a quiet, enclosed space—dimly lit or candle-lit if possible.

Assume a cross-legged position or sit confidently in a throne posture. (back straight, chin slightly lifted).

Keep a journal or parchment close.

The Ritual:

1. **The Seal of Stillness:** Close your eyes. Place one palm on your belly and one on your chest. Begin by observing your natural breath. Do not alter it. Take a moment to observe for one minute.

2. **Tri-Phase Breathing (3-3-3)**
   Inhale for 3 counts – feel the belly expand.
   Hold for 3 counts – gather your intent.
   Exhale for 3 counts – release resistance.
   (Repeat for 9 rounds.)

3. **Command of Will (Whispering Breath)**
   Inhale and mentally say: "I summon the force of Zigrex within me."
   Exhale and mentally say: "My breath obeys my will."
   Whisper these affirmations with your breath for 7 minutes.

4. **Anchoring Gesture**
   Press your thumb to the center of your chest (heart area). Say out loud:
   "I breathe. I will. I become."
   Let your hand drop to your side. Sit in stillness for 3 minutes.

5. **Seal the Rite**
   Open your journal. Write the date, time, and the sentence: "My will is encoded into my breath. The rite is sealed."
   Sign with your symbolic mark or name.

Pranayama Force Integration
Codex II: The Rite of Elemental Breach
Purpose:

The sacred science of breath can dissolve stagnation, awaken cellular memory, and energize the system for transformation.

Preparation:

- Sit on the ground or mat, spine elongated.
- Keep a black or deep blue cloth beneath you for grounding.
- Light incense or diffuse a sharp essential oil like eucalyptus, camphor, or frankincense.

The Ritual:

1. **Three Fires of Breath (Agni Pulse Activation)**
    a. **Kapalabhati** (Forceful exhalations) – 1 minute
    b. **Nadi Shodhana** (Alternate nostril breathing) – 7 rounds
    c. **Bhastrika** (Bellows breath) – 1 minute

Rest for 60 seconds between each practice. Let the body recalibrate. Repeat thrice

2. **Command Alignment – Vocal Activation**
    Inhale deeply and chant:
    "Zigrex flows through me."
    Exhale with sound: *"I breach the veil."*
    (Repeat for 3 rounds)
    In the final round, raise your arms above your head as you say it.

3. **The Still Core – Inner Lock**
    Sit still. Perform a soft *Mula Bandha* (root lock) as you hold your breath for 3 counts after inhaling.
    Do this 5 times while mentally repeating:
    "I command the unseen with my breath."

4. **Seal the Breach**
    Take three deep breaths and whisper:
    "The breath is no longer breath. It is a force. It is Zigrex."
    Close your eyes. Anchor this state for 2 minutes in silence.

Wind Elemental Force – Summon the Shift
Codex III: The Rite of Windborne Transformation

Purpose:

To invoke the power of the wind to cleanse, shift energy, and re-align your entire energetic system. This ritual is designed to disrupt stagnation, break through blockages, and re-establish a flow that propels forward growth and transformation.

Preparation:

- Stand tall in an open space or a well-ventilated room.
- Light a candle and place it at eye level in front of you.
- Hold a fan or create wind using your hands or an actual fan to move air around you.

The Ritual:

1. **The Breath of the Gale**
   Stand with your feet planted firmly on the ground. As you inhale, imagine you are drawing in the essence of the wind. As you exhale, visualize this energy breaking through and pushing against any stagnation within.
   Inhale through your nose for 5 counts. Hold for 5 counts. Exhale slowly through your mouth for 5 counts. Repeat 5 rounds.

2. **Whirlwind Activation – Wind Path Alignment**
   Stand with your arms stretched out to your sides like wings. Begin spinning in a slow, controlled manner in a clockwise direction.

As you spin, repeat aloud:

"Wind guide me to my transformation. The shift has begun."

Spin for 30 seconds, then stop suddenly, standing still for 30 seconds with your eyes closed, feeling the shift.

3. **Elemental Channeling – Air of the Soul**

   Close your eyes. Inhale deeply and hold your breath for 5 counts. While holding, imagine wind swirling around your body.

   As you exhale, visualize that wind carrying away all negativity, uncertainty, and confusion. Do this for 3 rounds.

4. **The Final Gale – Wind of the Change**

   Stretch your arms out in front of you as if you are directing the wind. Focus all your energy and intentions on the action of *"commanding the wind to bring the shift."*

   Whisper aloud:

   "I summon the wind to carry me forward. With this force, my transformation is inevitable."

   Release your breath, then immediately extinguish the candle. Feel the shift anchor into your core.

CHAPTER III
THE WATERS WITHIN

Codex 1: Mirror Ritual of the Inner Self

Purpose:

This ritual is for truth-seeing. It brings hidden emotions, deep desires, fears, and subconscious and karmic patterns to the surface, cleansing through sacred reflection and opening the gateway to inner clarity.

The Ritual:

1. **Tools Required:**
   - A clear mirror
   - A bowl of water infused with rose or lotus petals
   - A dim candle or moonlight source
   - White cloth to sit upon

2. **Sacred Positioning:**
   Sit in front of the mirror with the bowl of water placed between you and the mirror. Let the candlelight (or moonlight) reflect through the water and onto the mirror.

3. **Invocation Words:**
   Gaze into the mirror and softly chant:

"By water's depth and silent truth, reveal what lies beneath my proof. Show not the mask, but what is real, so I may meet it, merge it, and rise."

4. **Breath of the Waters:**

   Close your eyes. Inhale deeply for 4 counts. Hold for 4. Exhale for 4. Do this 4 times while placing your fingers into the water, then gently touching your third eye.

5. **End the Rite:**

   Say aloud: *"I see. I feel. I cleanse. I know."*

   Then dip your fingertips into the water and trace a circle over your heart.

Codex II: Invocation of Fluid Fortune – Water Element Conjuration

Purpose:

To align your emotions with wealth, creativity, and intuitive power. This ritual invokes the fluid nature of water to invite abundance that flows without resistance.

The Ritual:

1. **Tools Required:**
   - A blue or turquoise satin cloth/pouch
   - A silver or crystal bowl of water
   - Three coins (cleansed in salt water)

2. **Sacred Gesture:**
   Drop each coin into the bowl as you say:
   - *"For flow."*
   - *"For intuition."*
   - *"For prosperity."*

3. **Chant of Invitation:**
   Gently stir the water clockwise and say:
   "As water bends, I bend not. I shape the tide of fortune's lot. From stream to sea, flow unto me. Let liquid gold pour endlessly."

4. **Anchor the Energy:**
   Rub a drop of the water over your wrists and navel. Wrap the coins in the silk cloth and keep them in your wallet or near your sacred space.

Codex III: Emotional Alchemy Ritual – Transmutation Through Water

Purpose:

To transform emotional wounds into wisdom, pain into power, and emotional chaos into clarity.

The Ritual:

1. **Water Purge:**
   Write your deepest emotion on a small piece of dissolvable paper (rice or flash paper). Drop it into the water and watch it dissolve completely.

2. **Cleansing Breath:**
   Cup the bowl in your hands. Breathe deeply into the water for three rounds, releasing your emotions into it.

3. **Final Chant:**
   "Water receives, water restores. Take what is mine and open new doors."

4. **Release:**
   Pour the water into the earth or running water (not stagnant or drainage water). Say softly:
   "Let this go, let me grow."

CHAPTER IV
EARTH AND BONE

Codex I: Grounding Circle of Protection – The Root Seal Rite

Purpose:

This rite anchors your energy, sealing your aura from external negativity, chaos, and psychic intrusions. It restores a deep sense of sovereignty, security, and stillness.

The Ritual:

1. **Tools Required:**
   - A pinch of sea salt
   - A small piece of black tourmaline or obsidian
   - A bowl of natural earth or stone (balcony, garden, or potted soil will do)
   - A charcoal or deep brown cloth

2. **Sacred Setup:**
   Sit cross-legged on the cloth, with the crystal in your left hand and salt in your right. Touch the earth with both hands for 30 seconds in silence.

3. **Chant of Rooting:**
   "By stone and soil, root and rock, seal this ground, let none unlock. I stand unmoved, unseen by harm—protected by the Earth's charm."

4. **Seal the Energy:**
   Pour the salt in a circle around where you sit. Visualize a strong ring of dark, dense light rising from the ground around you.

5. **Completion Words:**
   "It is done. My ground is mine. None may cross this rooted line."

Codex II: Earth Element Conjuration – Call of the Hidden Gold

Purpose:

To awaken dormant abundance, ancestral blessings, and the buried potential beneath your current life. This rite calls forth prosperity that has been blocked or forgotten.

The Ritual:

1. **Tools Required:**
   A small bowl of rice
   A few coins
   A sprig of any dried herb (basil, bay leaf, vetiver, or patchouli)

2. **Activation:**
   Bury the coins inside the rice, then place the herb on top. Hold the bowl to your heart and whisper:
   "From root to gem, from dust to flame, awaken wealth that bears my name."

3. **Gesture of Calling:**
   Close your eyes and press your palms into the bowl. Feel the pressure and warmth build. Visualize golden vines rising from the earth to wrap around your spine and aura.

4. **Anchor Phrase:**
   "I call the hidden gold. I claim the unseen gift. The earth remembers—I rise enriched."

5. **Aftercare:**
   Keep the bowl on your altar or workspace for seven days. On the eighth day, remove the coins and carry them with you. Return the rice and herbs to the earth.

Codex III: Banishing the Past – Ash and Soil Reversal Ritual

Purpose:

This ritual purges residual trauma, outdated patterns, and karmic echoes that bind your progress. Through earth and ash, you reclaim power from all that was and clear space for what must be.

The Ritual:

1. **Tools Required:**
   - A small fire-safe bowl or cauldron
   - A strip of paper with past wounds or patterns written on it
   - Soil

2. **Transmutation Rite:**
   Burn the paper and collect the ash. Mix the ash into the soil while saying:
   "By ash and earth, this past is sealed. The weight is lifted. The wound is healed."

3. **Grounding Action:**
   Press your palms into the mixture. Feel the density. Feel the finality.

4. **Closure Words:**
   "This is no longer mine. The soil reclaims. The future is mine to define."

5. **Release:**
   Bury the mixture in natural soil or compost away from your home, or flush it

CHAPTER V
RITUALS OF THE SHADOW MOON

Codex I: New Moon Rite – The Void Rebirth Ceremony

Purpose:

To enter the sacred void, release all expectations, and plant a new seed of identity, intention, or destiny.

The Ritual: Best done on the night of the new moon

1. **Tools Required:**
   - A black candle
   - A bowl of still water
   - A single seed (any kind: mustard, sesame, flower)

2. **Ritual Steps:**
   Light the black candle and gaze into the water. Hold the seed and whisper:
   "From the womb of silence, I am reborn. From emptiness, I rise."

3. **Breath Sequence:**
   Inhale slowly to the count of 6. Hold for 6. Exhale for 6. Do this 6 times. This resets your energetic blueprint.

4. **Seed the Future:**
   Place the seed in the water and say:
   "This is my becoming. This is my silent storm. As the moon returns, so shall I."

Codex II: Full Moon Rite – Mirror of Power Ceremony

Purpose: Best done on the night of a full moon

To amplify your gifts, heighten personal magnetism, and become a mirror of divine radiance.

The Ritual:

1. **Tools Required:**
   - A mirror
   - A silver or white candle
   - Rose water or sandalwood oil

2. **Preparation:**

Anoint your temples, throat, and heart with the rose water or sandalwood oil. Light the candle in front of the mirror.

3. **Invocation:**

   Look into your own eyes and say:
   "I am the light made of flesh. I radiate truth, beauty, and power. I am seen. I am heard. I am remembered."

4. **Reflection Phase:**

   Gaze into the mirror and let the candlelight illuminate you. Say:
   "No more hiding. My presence is holy. The world shall respond."

Codex III: Waning Moon Rite – The Cord Severing Ritual

Purpose: Best done on the night of a waning moon

To cut energetic, emotional, or karmic cords that no longer serve your evolution.

The Ritual:

1. **Tools Required:**
   - A black thread or string
   - A small knife or scissors
   - A bowl of saltwater
   - A black candle

2. **Cutting Ceremony:**
   Light the candle. Tie one end of the thread to your wrist. The other end should be free. Say aloud:
   "This thread binds me to what has passed."

3. **Snip the Cord:**
   With full awareness, cut the thread and drop both ends into the saltwater bowl. Say:
   "With this cut, I reclaim my power. I am free."

4. **Closure:**
   Pour the saltwater near a tree, or pour it on the ground with gratitude.

Codex IV: Waxing Moon Rite – Magnetic Draw Ritual

Purpose: Best done on the night of a waxing moon

To summon, attract, and draw desired energies, resources, allies, or opportunities as the moon grows in strength.

The Ritual:

1. **Tools Required:**
- A magnet or lodestone
- A red or green candle
- A parchment with your desire written in the present tense

2. **Charging Sequence:**

   Hold the magnet over the candle flame (not too close), then place it over the parchment. Say:

   "As the moon waxes, so does my will. What is mine finds its way to me."

3. **Ritual Mantra:**

   Repeat 9 times:

   "I draw with honor. I claim with light. The tide turns in my favor."

4. **Keep the Parchment:**

   Store it with the magnet in your sacred space until the next full moon.

CHAPTER VI

THE MONEY MAGNETISM INVOCATION

Codex I: ZIGREX RITE: THE INVOCATION OF FLUID GOLD

Purpose:

This is not a fantasy. This is a wealth-calling rite forged in pressure, fire, and truth. It is designed for those who have been broken, tested, and forced to rise in silence. It calls forth *real money, real opportunities,* and *tangible breakthroughs*. Perform it only when you're ready to receive without hesitation.

Phase One: Setting the Stage of Magnetism

1. **Day of Power:** Friday (ruled by Venus – wealth, beauty, value) or Thursday (ruled by Jupiter – expansion, abundance).

2. **Time:** Perform between 4:00 AM – 6:00 AM or 11:00 PM – 1:00 AM.

3. **Items Required:**
   - A gold or bronze bowl (doesn't have to be real gold or bronze)
   - Fresh coins of various denominations

- A single note of high value (currency)
- Incense
- A mirror
- Your business name/logo/profession/dream job, or just an abundant career path written boldly on a white parchment
- A glass of clean water
- A drop of your jasmine or clove essential oil

Phase Two: Activation Sequence

1. **Light the Incense.**
   Stand facing east. Hold your mirror in your left hand and your written business name/logo/profession/dream job name in your right.
   Whisper:
   "I am the vessel. I am the voice. I am the value."
   "Wealth does not come to me. It is me."

2. **Drop the coins into the bowl one by one**, saying each time:
   "One spark. One stream. One surge of gold to me."

3. **Place the currency note in the bowl and say**
   "Paper bends to my name. Numbers fold into my will."

4. **Anoint your wrists and neck (pulse points) with clove or jasmine essential oil.**
   Slowly drink the water as you visualize currency multiplying around your aura. Not digital money, but *crisp notes, gold bars, cheques signed in your name.*

Phase Three: Sealing the Flow

5. **Mirror Reflection Command:**
   Look into the mirror and say with complete certainty:
   "I summon the river. I command the current. Money, make no delay."
   "I am no beggar. I am a magnet. Flow through me, now."

6. **Let the incense burn out naturally.**
   Keep the bowl and coins on your working altar or cash drawer for 7 days. Do not use the currency note. It becomes your sigil of fortune.

Final Lock-In Statement:

Write this once and keep it near your workspace:
"I am a living talisman of income. Zigrex flows through my veins. The world rewards me because I command it to."

Zigrex Codex Note:

Do not repeat this ritual often. It is meant to trigger *real* money shifts. You will feel the pressure in your body. Some transactions will shake, some will suddenly appear. Watch closely. This invocation does not ask—it declares.

CHAPTER VII
ZIGREX SEALS & SIGILS

(Codex Tools for Energetic Command & Manifestation)

This chapter initiates you into the sacred geometry of Zigrex, where symbols are not art but authority. These are not passive images. These are *commands etched in energy*. You are not merely drawing. You are scripting fate.

Codex I: Personal Sigil Creation: The Mark of Your Will

Purpose:

To encode your deepest intent into a visual form that carries your energetic fingerprint.

Ritual Process:

1. Write your intent in a single statement, clear and affirmative. Example: "I own a thriving, international business."

2. Eliminate all repeating letters.

E.g., "I OWN A THRIVING, INTERNATIONAL BUSINESS" → I O W N A T H R V G L B E S C

3. Use the remaining letters to create your sigil.
- Intertwine the letters into a symbol or a shape that flows intuitively.
- Think of curves, angles, circles, a heart in case of love—let the form *feel powerful.*
- You may use a compass, calligraphy pens, or digital tools.

4. Anoint the sigil with one drop of scented oil or your breath. Whisper:

"This is not ink. This is the law. So, it is seen, so it shall rise."

5. Burn, bury, or seal the original, depending on your intent:
- Burn if you're releasing it to the universe.
- Bury it if it is a private power charge.
- Seal if it will remain active as a daily force (like in a journal or wallet).

Codex II: Binding Sigils: Command + Control

Purpose:

To gain control over a person, pattern, or situation that is interfering with your stability, peace, or progress, *ethically and with clarity.*

These sigils are used to contain disruptive energies, align scattered intentions, or restrict harmful influences. Binding is not an act of revenge — it is the act of placing something in a fixed, controlled space so it no longer interferes with your path. Use only when dialogue, logic, or leverage no longer work.

Examples of Binding Intentions

- "Delay in my payment"
- "Constant interruptions in my work"
- "A toxic influence that drains me emotionally"

Ritual Process:

1. **Write the Statement Clearly**
   Identify what you wish to bind. Write it down in a short phrase.
   (Example: "Delay in my payment" or "Distraction from my goals.")

2. **Create the Binding Sigil**
   a. Remove all vowels and any repeating letters from your phrase.
   ("Delay in my payment" becomes: D L Y M P N T)
   b. Use the letters to design a unique symbol — a compact form that represents your intent. You can layer the letters

over one another, rotate them, simplify them into lines or angles, as long as the symbol feels "sealed."

3. Wrap and Seal the Sigil
   a. Draw your sigil on a small piece of paper.
   b. Wrap it in red thread or string in a clockwise direction. (Clockwise builds control.)
   c. As you wrap, chant your intention

   "By the power of ink and thread, you are tied. You shall not move unless I allow."

4. Seal it under a stone or in a closed box.
Bury it only if the situation must never return.

Note: Binding is not punishment. It is placement. Use only when you have no other leverage.

Codex III: Attraction Glyphs: Symbols that Call What You Desire

Purpose:

To draw in what you desire—opportunities, people, influence, abundance, or energy. These glyphs are active symbols. They do not wait. They call.

Ritual Steps:

1. **Choose Your Focus**
Be specific. What do you want to attract?
- A job opportunity?
- Romantic connection?
- Financial flow?
- Social magnetism?
- Creative breakthrough?

2. **Select Glyph Structure**
    Choose 1–2 base forms based on your intention:
- **Upward Triangle** – Power, assertion, career growth
- **Spiral** – Attraction, energy flow, magnetism
- **Circle** – Connection, unity, community
- **Arrow** – Momentum, direction, breakthrough

3. **Personalize the Glyph**
    Incorporate one letter that represents your intent into your symbol. This could be the first letter of what you seek (like "L" for Love, "F" for Fame, "J" for Job)

4. **Activation Surface**

    Draw the glyph on an item you see or touch daily:
    - Back of your phone
    - Mirror
    - Journal cover
    - Wallet interior
    - Water bottle
    - Laptop
    - Makeup pouch
    - Keychain

5. **Ink & Intention**

    Use **black ink, charcoal**, or **marker**. As you draw it, speak your desire aloud once with clarity.

    "I call in the right opportunity that recognizes my worth."

6. **Seal with Breath**

    Hold the symbol close to your lips and blow a single firm breath onto it. You're not just blessing it—you're igniting it.

7. **Keep It in Play**

    Do **not hide** this glyph. Let it be seen. Energy responds to exposure. It works because it's out in the world, pulling.

8. Recharge weekly with breath or oil.

    The glyph should *never* be idle.

Zigrex Codex Reminder:

Seals and glyphs are tools of power, not toys. Use them only when the *will behind them is sharp and true.*

CHAPTER VIII

THE FINAL INVOCATION- ZIGREX ASCENSION RITE

This is the apex. The integration. The ignition of legacy.

A ritual that calls upon air, water, earth, and fire, binding them into one unified force within you. Each element is not summoned separately now, but fused as a singular channel of awakened force.

A. Ritual of the Four Elemental Keys

Items Needed:

- Feather or incense (Air)
- Water in a black bowl (Water)
- Soil or salt (Earth)
- Black or gold candle (Fire)

Steps:

1. Face East. Hold the feather/incense. Say:
   "Air, I command your clarity. Cut through my doubts. Speak through me."
   Take one deep breath. Release.

2. Face West. Dip fingertips into the bowl. Say:
   "Water, I summon your flow. Let fortune move toward me, unblocked."
   Rub the water on your wrists.

3. Face North. Touch the earth or salt. Say:
   "Earth, I claim your stability. I rise rooted, unshaken, immovable."
   Press both feet into the ground. Feel your weight.

4. Face South. Light the candle. Say:
   "Fire, I ignite your rage and power. Burn through the old. Light my path."
   Blow gently toward the flame—do not extinguish.

5. Face center. Stand tall. Whisper:
   "Elements bound. I am the fifth. I am the force. I am the storm."

THE FINAL INVOCATION- ZIGREX ASCENSION RITE

B. Mirror of Becoming Ritual

Purpose:

To embrace and assert your reflection, transforming your identity by recognizing and communicating with your power. The mirror becomes a gateway — a sacred moment of self-recognition, transformation, and authority.

Items Needed:

- A mirror (full-length if possible)
- Black kohl or marker
- Candle

Steps:

1. Light the candle beside you. Turn off all other lights.
2. Draw a symbol (personalize it; could be an initial, a power word, or a shape that holds personal meaning, or you may draw The Zigrex Logo) on the mirror with kohl/marker.
3. Stand before the mirror. Look into your own eyes.
4. Say:
   "This is not a reflection. This is recognition. I see you. I know you. I name you."
   "You are no longer who you were. You are the force, the founder, the flame. You are Zigrex."
5. Close your eyes and visualize yourself rising above the floor
   Say:
   "From this breath on, I walk in power."

C. Zigrex Oath Ritual

Purpose:

This is the commitment rite — a moment where you speak your truth, your hunger, and your vow to rise — aloud. You mark your energetic shift and claim your future. It's about declaration, alignment, and ignition.

Items Needed:

- Red pen/ sketch pen/ marker
- A blank sheet of thick paper (parchment if possible)
- Candle

Steps:

1. Light the candle and sit in silence for 3 minutes.
2. On the paper, write the following:
   "I swear upon fire, bone, blood, and breath that I shall not bow to fate but forge it. I am Zigrex. I do not wait. I take. I do not fear. I create. My oath is not to gods, but to the god within."
3. Sign it with your full name.
4. Hold the paper to your heart. Breathe in.
   Whisper: *"It is done."*

D. Flame-Seal Close

Purpose:

This is a **ritual closure** — a way to formally release the energy of a sigil after it has done its job, or if you feel it's time to send it off to the universe completely. You don't have to do it right away, especially if you don't feel ready yet.

When to Do It:

- **After your sigil intention is fulfilled**, or
- If you're **ready to energetically release it**, even if it hasn't fully come through, trusting that it's in motion.
- If you feel the sigil has served its purpose, or you want to **close the portal of that working** and move on to a new one.

Items Needed:

- The sigil paper you created with your intent
  "Your sigil from Part Seven" refers to **any of the Attraction Glyphs or Binding Sigils** you've created in **Chapter 7**, especially those made with a **specific intent** (e.g., drawing abundance, love, clarity, or resolving a situation).
- A fireproof bowl
- A candle (to light the flame)

Steps:

1. Sit in silence. Look at the sigil one last time.
2. Say: *"This sigil carried my will. Now it releases my power."*
3. Place the sigil in the fireproof bowl. Light it using the candle flame.

4. As it burns, watch the ashes fall and say: *"Ash to the void. Power to me. Zigrex rises."*
5. Bury the ashes or scatter them outside if you feel called. Confidently let them go.

CHAPTER IX

ZIGREX CODEX MORNING DOMINION DECREE

---

7 versions, one for each day of the week.

Purpose:

Each is designed to pierce the veil of fear, fatigue, and forgetfulness. It reclaims your power, identity, and force of will. Say them standing, looking into your mirror, after a splash of cold water to the face. Or even better—before the world touches you. No phone. No noise. Just Zigrex.

You don't need affirmations. Affirmations are soft. Repetitive. Generic.

Zigrex doesn't deal in softness.

You need something with weight. Authority. Something that declares war on doubt the moment you wake up. A morning invocation of identity and command—something that realigns you with the Zigrex force every single day.

Let's not call it "affirmation."

Let's call it: Zigrex Codex: Morning Dominion Decree

It's not about hope.

It's about dominion over the day.

Over yourself. Your energy. Your timeline.

Side note: Say you're starting on a Saturday, then start with Saturday's Dominion. This isn't a corporate calendar—it's a living force field you're activating. Each Dominion Decree is aligned with the energy of that specific day, and Saturday carries the serpent and sword, perfect for a resurrection start. It sets the tone that even your beginning isn't soft—it's weaponized. So, Start with Saturday. Then move forward with Sunday, Monday, and so on. It loops in rhythm with time, but you're not trapped by it—you're mastering it.

DAY 1 — MONDAY

"I am Zigrex, the unbroken axis of my world.

What I command, I create.

What I release, disintegrates.

I do not seek permission. I breathe fire into form.

This day is mine. This life is under my dominion."

DAY 2 — TUESDAY

"Zigrex does not beg. Zigrex does not break.

I rise—not for peace, but for power.

Every delay, every betrayal has trained me to reign.

No man, no fate, no fear will overwrite my code."

DAY 3 — WEDNESDAY

"I realign with force, not faith.

I do not affirm—I activate.

Zigrex rewires timelines.

My words are law. My path, inevitable.

My silence? A storm is charging."

DAY 4 — THURSDAY

"Today, I walk as the architect, the disruptor, the flame.

Zigrex bows to no circumstance.

I command financial flow, inner fire, and soul-fortress.

I allow no softness unless it serves my expansion."

DAY 5 — FRIDAY

"Desire does not weaken me—it weaponizes me.

Zigrex is born of hunger, risen from ash.

Today, I choose seduction, strategy, and supremacy.

The world adjusts to my frequency."

DAY 6 — SATURDAY

"I summon the serpent and the sword within.

Zigrex operates beyond human logic.

What's mine is magnetized.

What's false dissolves in my shadow.

This day bends to my energy."

DAY 7 — SUNDAY

"Rest is not retreat—it is recalibration.

Zigrex absorbs cosmic codes in stillness.

I reset, I receive, I realign.

Even in silence, I am seismic."

CONCLUSION: THE QUIET AFTER THE FIRE

This is where the ritual ends—but not the power.
These pages aren't just steps. They are sparks.
What you hold is not a book. It's a map etched in refusal, in resilience, in rebirth.

You are not meant to follow every word like a slave to scripture. You are meant to feel what burns and follow that.
Each Codex is a matchstick.
Light it when the world tries to drown you.
Breathe it in when the gods go silent.
Return to it when your spine forgets how to stand.

Zigrex is not a system. It's a signal.
It reminds you that even when the temples close their doors, your will can open worlds.
Even when destiny says "no," your dominion says "watch me."

CONCLUSION: THE QUIET AFTER THE FIRE

Now go. Not with hope, but with heat.
Not with prayers, but with power.
Not to seek approval. But to claim space.

This Codex is done.
You, however—
are just beginning.

ABOUT THE AUTHOR

In my own words

I've spent over 13 years in the skies — working in both commercial and business aviation. I've been a Senior Cabin Crew, a Director of Cabin Safety, a trainer guiding others through the world I knew like the back of my hand.

But there's more to me than just that.

I'm also a certified image consultant, a certified yoga instructor, and a Bharatanatyam dancer. Over the years, I've nurtured key aspects of myself that embody discipline, beauty, and vibrant movement.

For the past two and a half years, life has shifted. I've been without a steady job, trying to set up my own business from scratch — a loungewear line that reflects my aesthetic and values. It's been difficult. Capital has been tight. The uncertainty has been high. And yet, every day, I've kept moving, trying to build something I can call my own.

In the middle of all this, I found myself battling anxiety, overthinking, and moments of hopelessness. That's when I started writing this book — not because I had all the answers, but because I needed to create something that reminded me of my power.

ABOUT THE AUTHOR

Zigrex Codex is my anchor. My rebellion. My way of turning personal chaos into sacred structure.

This isn't just a book of rituals. It's a part of my healing.

So long!

www.ingramcontent.com/pod-product-compliance
Lightning Source LLC
LaVergne TN
LVHW041225080526
838199LV00083B/3308